THINGS PHOTOGRAPHERS Really WANT TO Say But Can't

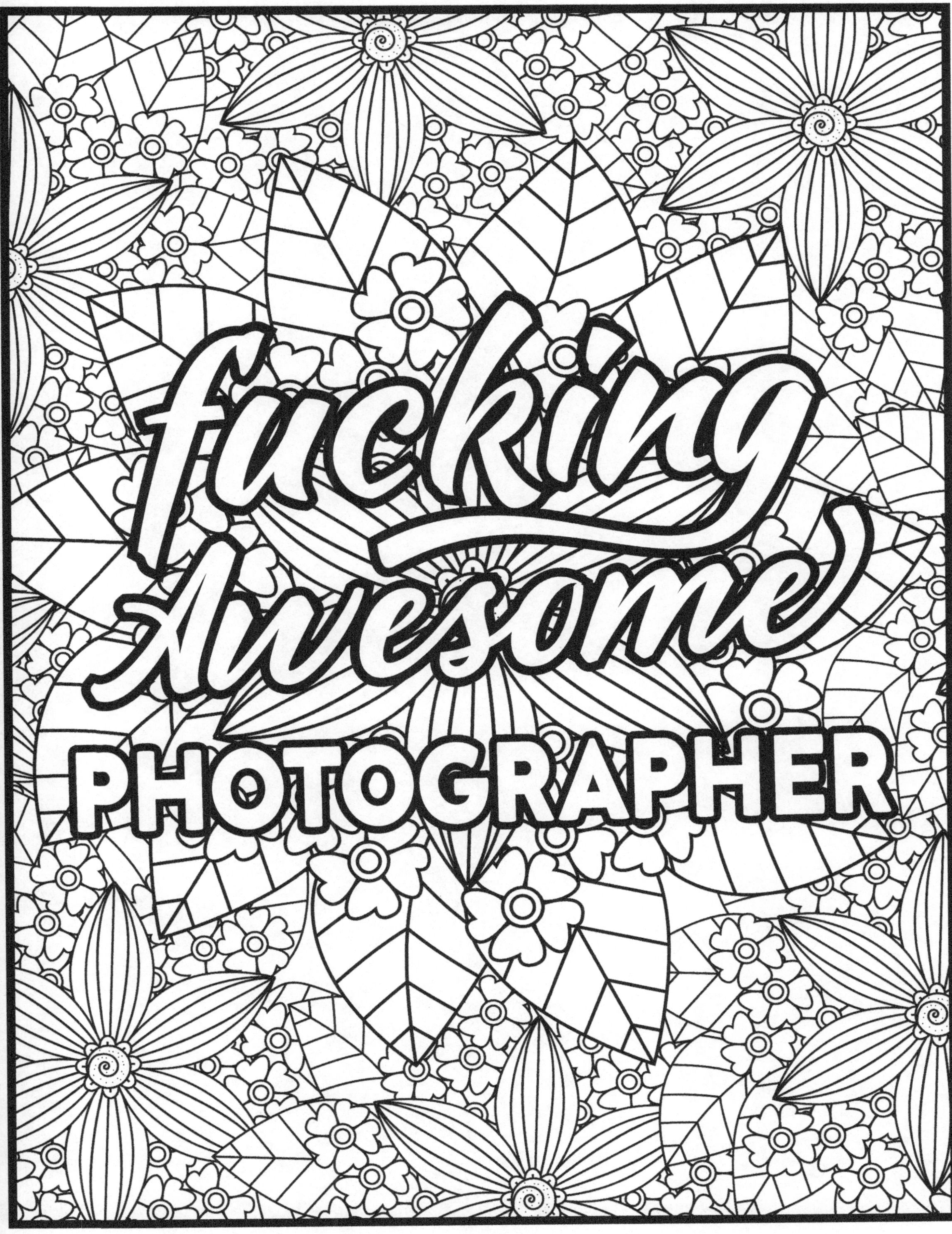
fucking Awesome
PHOTOGRAPHER

You Are
AMAZING
As Fuck

be Happy
EVERY
damn
DAY!

I'm A
PHOTOGRAPHER
Not a
Fucking
Magician

I Can &
I FUCKING
Will

WAKE UP.
Kick Some
FUCKING ASS.
Repeat.

YOU
FUCKIN'
GOT THIS

Now
or
Never

Today Is the
MOTHER FUCKING
Day

Keep
life
simple

FUCK OFF!
IT'S HOME
TIME

Hey
you're
FUCKING
Great

SCREW YOU!

That Ain't
MY FUCKING
Problem

Fuck
Perfect

fucking
GREAT
PHOTOGRAPHER

Too Calm
TO GIVE A
Damn

WAKE UP
AND BE A
Fucking
AWESOME

Be Strong
BELIEVE in YOURSELF

Be the Light
You're amazing

SMILE MORE.
WORRY
FUCKING
LESS!

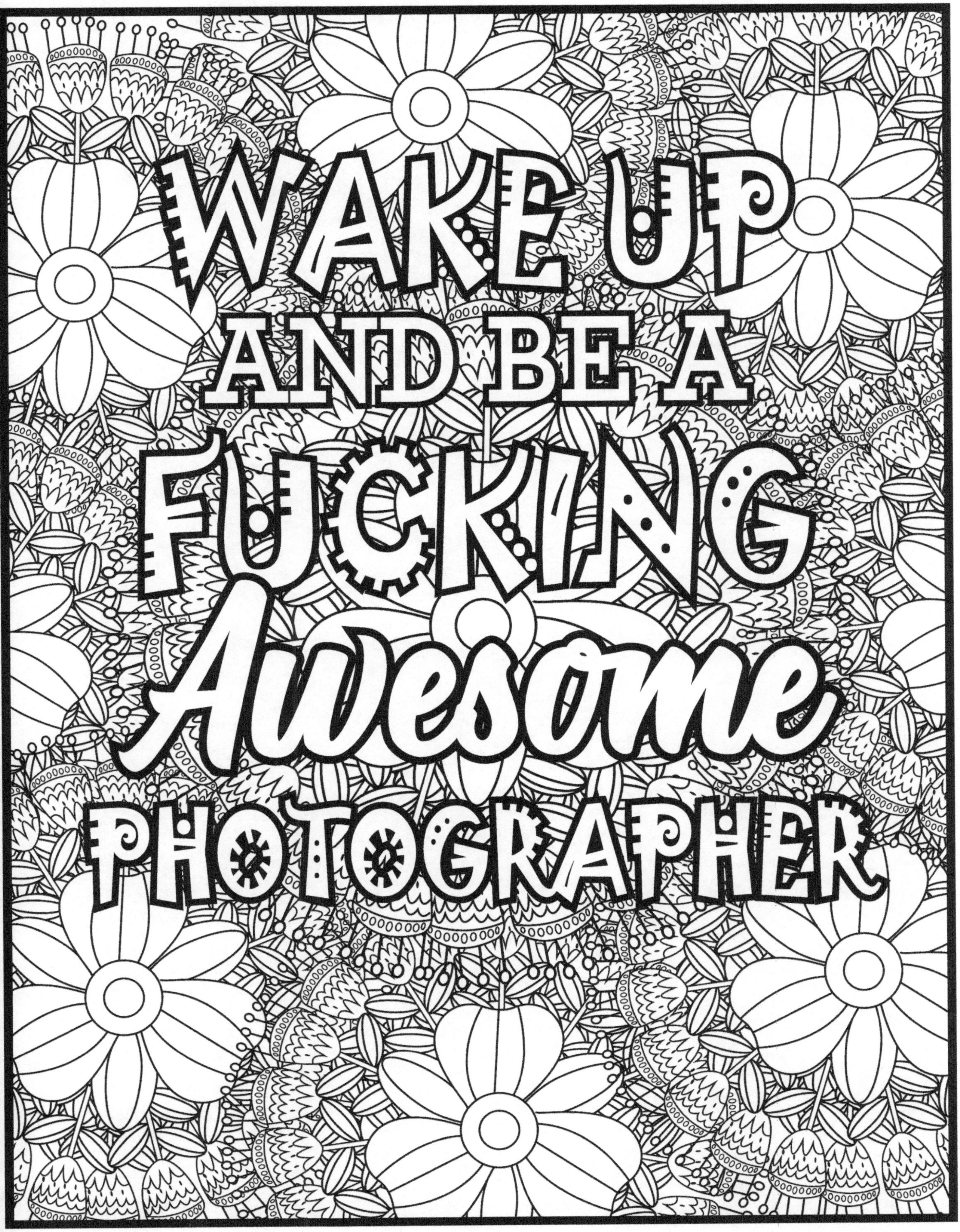
WAKE UP
AND BE A
FUCKING
Awesome
PHOTOGRAPHER

opportunities
Are All
AROUND
ME

Spread Love
EVERYWHERE
YOU FUCKING
Go

YOU ARE
Awesome As
FUCK

Let That
Shit
go

You Are
A FUCKING
Rock

be happy
IT DRIVES
ASSHOLES
Crazy

Cheer
The
Fuck
Up

TAKE NO
SHITS.
GIVE NO
FUCKS.

I Gave
Zero
Fucks
Today

SLAY ALL
MOTHER
FUCKING
DAY

CALM THE
Fuck Down
&
Color

Hey
Fuckface
Do Some
Work

Dealing
WITH YOUR
BULLSHIT
ISN T IN MY JOB
Description

The Best
is yet to
FUCKING
COME

I'm A Kind
OF A
FUCKING
GREAT
Deal

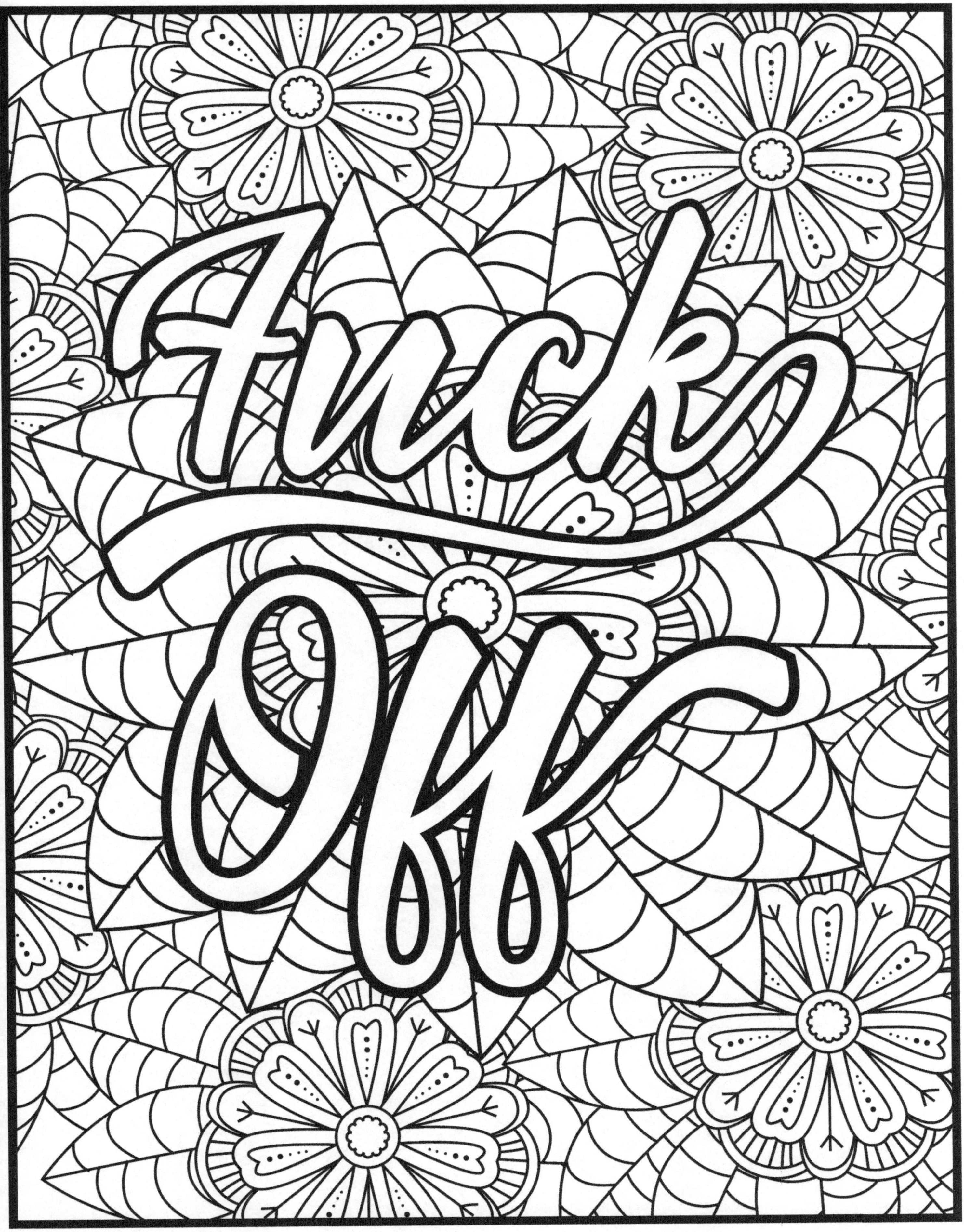
Fuck
Off

Test Your Colors

Made in the USA
Monee, IL
10 October 2023

44366652R00046